"'Leave a legacy? Me?' If you have not addressed these questions—or even if you think you have—you need to read Pat Renn's book. It is an easy read that addresses the whys and hows to make sure you maximize the assets you accumulate over your lifetime. Today is the right time!"

Dr. David Apple Jr.,
medical director emeritus of the Shepherd Center

"Pat has been a longtime supporter of Special Olympics Georgia. His many contributions include valuable guidance to help establish and grow the organization's investment account, countless volunteer hours at various events, and spreading awareness and information about the incredible athletes that we serve. We appreciate Pat's commitment to the 26,702 children and adults with intellectual disabilities registered in the program and know that he is a true fan of all of the athletes."

Georgia Milton-Sheats,
CEO of Special Olympics Georgia

"Every person has been put on Earth for a purpose greater than themselves, which means that your wealth is greater than your money. Pat Renn has done a terrific job in his latest book of finding the greater purpose of your money. Take time to read it. Better yet, take time to act on it."

Scott Keffer,

best-selling author, coach, and the

creator of *The Donor Motivation Program*

All of the proceeds from sales of

Finding Your Money's Greater Purpose

will be donated to charity.

---

*"The true meaning of life is to plant a tree,
under whose shade you do not expect to sit"...*
–Nelson Henderson

FINDING YOUR
MONEY'S
GREATER PURPOSE

FINDING YOUR
MONEY'S
GREATER PURPOSE

How to Make Your Legacy Count

PATRICK RENN

Published by Advantage, Charleston, South Carolina.
Member of Advantage Media Group.

ADVANTAGE is a registered trademark and the Advantage colophon is a trademark of Advantage Media Group, Inc.

Printed in the United States of America.

ISBN: 978-159932-579-8
LCCN: 2015936609

Advantage Media Group is proud to be a part of the Tree Neutral® program. Tree Neutral offsets the number of trees consumed in the production and printing of this book by taking proactive steps such as planting trees in direct proportion to the number of trees used to print books. To learn more about Tree Neutral, please visit www.treeneutral.com. To learn more about Advantage's commitment to being a responsible steward of the environment, please visit www.advantagefamily.com/green

Advantage Media Group is a publisher of business, self-improvement, and professional development books and online learning. We help entrepreneurs, business leaders, and professionals share their Stories, Passion, and Knowledge to help others Learn & Grow. Do you have a manuscript or book idea that you would like us to consider for publishing? Please visit advantagefamily.com or call 1.866.775.1696.

*To my wife, Suzi, who has made life worth living,
while I was busy making a living.
To my two sons, Tyler and Owen, who have exhibited great
patience while I learned parenting skills on the job.
To Lynn Carter, my colleague for many years
who was taken from us much too early.
To my present staff, Kathryn Edmunds and Laura Martin,
who define what it means to care about the client.
To all who toil daily in the pursuit of the greater good.*

FOREWORD

Over the last 25 years, I have watched Pat Renn go from being a young, eager financial planner, to a seasoned expert and sought-after resource in the Atlanta area for building a legacy through charitable giving.

Pat has used his own life story to capture the salient points that you need to know about how financial and estate planning can be enhanced by charitable giving. He makes it very clear that the key is having approachable advisors who ask the right questions and work as a team to fulfill your needs and objectives.

This book shows you the "Why" so that you can determine the "What" when it comes to finding your money's greater purpose through charitable giving. Pat urges everyone to develop a clear "Lifeprint" to follow during their lives and leave as a legacy for the people, the causes, and the institutions they care about. He effectively confronts any fear or insecurity you have about running out of money before you die through careful planning with the assistance of his network of knowledgeable advisors. Just like he does in his practice, Pat's book emphasizes the importance of asking questions, the necessity of patient listening, and the use of storytelling to illustrate important concepts that you need to know.

Once you and your family have built adequate funds for your future and make the conscious decision to take the steps to make your legacy count, this book will show you the ways that charitable gifts can be made in the most tax-efficient manner. This book is an excellent starting point if you want to make these desires a reality.

Harry Lamon, JD, CLU, ChFC, AEP,
retired tax and employee benefits attorney and life member of the
Metro Atlanta and National Salvation Army Advisory Boards

TABLE OF CONTENTS

ABOUT THE AUTHOR

Patrick G. Renn is the founder and president of the Renn Wealth Management Group, Inc. He is a Certified Financial Planner™ professional with more than 35 years of experience in providing financial counseling to high-net-worth individuals, business owners, and professionals.

Pat is the former president of the Georgia Society of the Institute of Certified Financial Planners and former president of the Georgia chapter of the International Association for Financial Planning. He is currently a member of the Society of Financial Services Professionals, the Atlanta Estate Planning Council, and the Georgia Planned Giving Council. He holds a bachelor's degree in business administration from Villanova University and an MBA from Loyola College. He holds the Advanced Pension Planning certificate from the American College as well as the Investment Management Consultant designation from Raymond James Institute.

Pat served on the board of trustees of Holy Innocents' Episcopal School and was chair of its Endowment Funds

Committee. Pat also served as chair of the Cathedral of St. Philip Endowment Funds and is the current chair of the Episcopal Media Center Endowment. He is past board chair of the Georgia Special Olympics and has served on numerous charitable and professional boards.

Pat is married with two sons. He enjoys travel, golf, fly fishing, and wing shooting in his spare time.

Patrick G. Renn
prenn@rennwealth.com

The Renn Wealth Management Group, Inc.
3205 Paces Ferry Place, NW
Atlanta, Georgia 30305
(T) 404-467-9882 (F) 404-467-9104

INTRODUCTION

ONE FOR ALL

At an Atlanta Hawks basketball game that I attended one day in the mid-1980s, the halftime was the highlight.

Several young people from the Special Olympics took to the court, and as they played, I put my arms around the shoulders of my two little boys next to me in the stands. I looked at those young Olympians on the court, putting all their heart into the game despite the disabilities with which they no doubt struggled every day.

They performed with aplomb, and yet I found myself thinking of the old expression, "There but for the grace of God go I." It was not that I was looking down on them, as if I were somehow better or more favored. What I felt was a desire to be worthy of their looking up to me.

At halftime, my neighbor gave a presentation about the Special Olympics. I called him later, and he invited me to get involved. I ended up on the Special Olympics board for a number of years, eventually chairing it and helping to develop an endowment fund.

For several years, my boys and I would attend summer and winter games at college campuses. We would stay overnight and volunteer at the competitions. The atmosphere of excitement was palpable as those athletes showed their parents, their families, and the world just what they were made of and just what they had to share.

I wanted my children to see that each and every one of us can make a meaningful contribution to helping our fellow human beings and that this experience can drive home the lesson that they must never prejudge people.

One thing about being around special children like those athletes is they have a spirit that is tender and friendly and non-threatening. They're very open individuals. Unlike a lot of folks who were on the board, I had not been personally involved with Special Olympics competitions before. But I have long believed that young people develop life skills and an appreciation of teamwork from being involved in sports. I admire the program for giving those with special challenges an opportunity to enjoy that experience. It is their moment to be a winner, to hear the cheers, to feel victorious even against great odds.

It's not just the athletes who gain something but the community at large as well. In years past, these folks, typically, were kept on the sidelines and were not very visible in the community. I would like to think our society has advanced far beyond that. A lot of that change is attributable to the dedicated and diligent work of volunteers who strive for something better for us all, and I am grateful for whatever small role I have been able to play in that evolution.

I believe the sports experience teaches you, as a participant, volunteer, sponsor, or spectator, that those who have such challenges in life have goals and ambitions like the rest of us.

The Special Olympics has its roots in a summer day camp started by Eunice Kennedy Shriver in the early 1960s at her home in suburban Washington. Mental disabilities had become a priority issue of the Kennedy administration, which understood such a challenge because the president's sister, Rosemary, had long been institutionalized with mental disabilities.

The family possessed the kind of influence and leadership that made things happen. Under the direction of Sargent and Eunice Shriver, the Special Olympics did much to advance the acceptance of people with mental disabilities. The Shrivers had discovered the power of sports to unify and engender acceptance.

OUR QUEST FOR SIGNIFICANCE

Each of us, through our contributions as volunteers and benefactors, holds the power to change the course of society for the better. We can leave our mark on this world with the time and the resources that we dedicate to others. That is what becomes our legacy.

This concept is not unique to me. Ernest Becker wrote a book titled *The Denial of Death*, in which he stated that "man fears not so much extinction as extinction without significance." I think we all desire to leave our print on the people, causes, or institutions we care about. To do that, we don't have to leave a substantial financial legacy to a university, as nice as that would be. It can be as simple as the effect we have on other people while we're around, what we've done to further a cause that we care about, or what we've done to make sure an institution we care about not only survives but flourishes and endures.

I have a warm spot in my heart for my high school. I learned a lot of important life skills there and came to understand what's important and what's not. I am not sure I realized that at the time, but as I go through life and look back, I consider those four years to have been highly worthwhile.

For most of us, appreciating the life lessons we learn at school comes much later, as we think back. I do not know that I would change much of anything in my life. I can't think of many experiences, positive or negative, that have not had an effect on me or somehow benefited me. I've had great experiences all my life. It is only as you get a little bit older that you think of those times with gratitude.

I was a younger man when I was involved with the Special Olympics. I was wrapped up in my career. I had young children and a mortgage and was focused on doing my best for my family. Yet, the experience helped me to understand that people who are very different from me can be accepted for no reason other than their humanity.

A GRATEFUL ATTITUDE

When it is my time to leave this earth, I hope that one or two causes or institutions might be doing all the better because of whatever impact I had on them. And I want to help others do the same.

I've discovered, in working with others, that a lot of people are of the same mind. In one way or another they feel indebted, if not truly grateful. As a result, many have become community builders.

Sure, we can find much to complain about. But here we are. We can ask ourselves what we can do that might make things a little bit better. Involvement with a hospital or school or the arts, all of that is helpful in building our communities. Many are interested in contributing a portion of the resources with which they have been blessed to support the people and causes they have come to admire: their faith, their schools, and their communities and the many institutions within them.

I think such contributions are natural. Whenever I hear people say such things as "I feel fortunate," "I feel blessed," and "I feel that a lot of doors have been opened for me," I know I am tapping into those sentiments. When I hear those words, I know that we're probably going to communicate well. If I hear

FINDING YOUR MONEY'S GREATER PURPOSE

"I did it all myself," however, or "Nobody gave me a thing," that's another track.

It is a matter of attitude. People often are grateful just for the opportunity. We know when we have been fortunate. I could have been born in a hut somewhere and grown up having to worry about bullets flying over my head. Most of the people whom I deal with have that attitude of gratitude. They feel some responsibility to improve their lot and help others become all that they can be.

Such is the case with the Special Olympians. They're trying to run the race. In one way or another, many people are trying to run the race as best they know how or are able. A lot of them need help.

THE CONFIDENCE TO DO MORE

Many people feel that doors have been opened for them, and they want to open doors for others, to give back, and yet, they do not, for one reason or another. They do less than they could.

I feel that part of my mission is to show those people that there is more they could do without financially jeopardizing themselves or their family. In other words, they could take advantage of certain financial procedures, if only they knew about them. With a bit of planning, such procedures could benefit not only them but also the causes and institutions they care about.

My objective in planned giving is to leave the benefactors and their families better off financially. They can gain strength through giving. Many people do not understand that.

People with a charitable interest have the opportunity to develop it further. They all have what we call social capital, money they will not get to keep. It is legislated to go to taxes, but it could be used to benefit charity. That is an option. How that's done is part of what I am about.

To develop that opportunity sometimes requires building confidence. People have that seed within them, that desire to do something for the benefit of others, but they worry first about whether they themselves are going to be okay. They need reassurance. I help them see they could do good for this world without sacrificing their own lifestyle or reducing what they can leave to their own families.

Before giving comes clarity. Once people clearly understand their situation, they gain the confidence to act. Confidence is the main ingredient people need to be turned on to the concept of giving. My role is to help instill that confidence in them.

AT THE CORE IS CALCULATION

Whether people have a lot of money or a little, there are three primary questions on their minds: Do I have enough? Will I still have enough? Who or what is most worthy of my money?

The answer to those first two questions—Do I have enough? Will I still have enough?—is a financial calculation that is the essence of financial planning. You can project the figures. You can make some assumptions, and you can adjust year by year. The answer is either yes or no. If you do not have enough, how can you compensate so that you will? As things come up you did not anticipate, what effect do they have? If things go better than expected, what impact do they have?

The third question—Who or what is most worthy of my money?—is the one that most people need a little help with. That is the subjective part, the advisory part, the counseling part that we help people come to conclusions about. They want to figure out not only who deserves their contributions and why they deserve them but also how much they should give and in what manner.

Again, at its core, it is a calculation, but it is also about making a value statement: Here's what's important to me. I want to make sure that I leave my children and grandchildren enough. I would like to make that available, and I could use some help to know how much that is. Beyond that, I care about certain institutions, and I want to be sure that I become part of their success.

That all can be quantified, but first, we need to discuss and discover the values that the individual, or couple, holds dear. Once we see what is important to them, we can put numbers around it.

<u>ONE PERSON AT A TIME</u>

We're on a journey. I work with people who are trying to figure out what they are capable of doing. Once they are confident and reassured of that, they can decide where they want to go with that beautiful thought. They can determine how they might become a benefactor or philanthropist.

Each of us has had unique experiences in life. We've had causes that we have believed in. We have had people who have helped us. There comes a time in life for many of us when we want to open those doors for others. I know that has been the case for me. I've had certain advantages and opportunities, and I would love to be able to make those available to others.

I have a friend, a successful businessman, who has retired. He went to Georgia Tech on a scholarship and now provides scholarships to students. Once the students are selected each year, my friend mentors them through all four years at Georgia Tech, through graduate school, and into their early business career. People find that kind of close involvement to be incredibly satisfying.

That particular benefactor, though he came from very modest circumstances, did very well financially. He has a long track record of success. He was an Eagle Scout who went to Georgia Tech and to Harvard Business School. He still serves on a couple of business boards.

He felt the desire to get to know these scholarship recipients personally and has had a significant influence on their lives. One person at a time, he is making his mark on the world.

THE DESIRE TO GIVE BACK

This focus of mine developed as a result of my taking a look at my client base some years ago. A good friend in the business told me that the secret to marketing was to find people who thought the same way I did, do business with them, and eliminate the others. As all good marketing people will tell you, stick with your own kind, so to speak. That is, understand where these folks are coming from, look for what they have in common, and determine what distinguishes your practice from that of every other certified financial planner out there.

I discovered that many of my clients had a desire to give back but were uncertain of the next steps to take. We had been involved in helping them develop their philanthropic planning because they all needed some help with it. Many sat on charitable boards, and some chaired large capital campaigns; they were known and respected in the community for those sorts of things. It took me a while to figure out the details, but the pattern was unmistakable.

I had been involved in a number of charitable boards and endowment boards and had never solicited anyone for any of that type of personal financial planning service. But as a result of my helping organizations in that area, board members would approach me and ask if I could help with personal matters.

I enjoyed working with them. They were pleasant people who had their priorities in order and were doing some effective things in the community. So, that's how my planning practice developed. From those experiences, I developed into the guy you could sit down with and explore your philanthropic options.

I believe this book will be helpful to anyone who wants to explore the desire to give back. And I think it will be helpful to other advisors who have the same focus and passion that I do. I also think it would be helpful to the people at charitable institutions who talk every day to potential donors about their many concerns.

TO DONORS AND CHARITIES ALIKE

The purpose of this book is to reach out to charities and donors that need to understand what is possible. I want to help them make the most of the contributions they make and receive. I want to see as much of their money as possible reach the intended target.

Though we focus on people with resources above a certain level, I'll talk to anybody who has an interest in giving of themselves. Perhaps, I can offer some ideas pro bono. Those who become our clients tend to have significant assets. Typically, they have first-generation wealth. They made their money through business or a profession. About a third of them are widows. Another third are retired, and the remainder are still working and building their net worth. Most have a desire to get involved, at some level, in philanthropic planning.

I have found that I can help most charities that have relatively modest financial resources but highly worthwhile causes. The major, venerable institutions such as Harvard are going to be just fine because their value to posterity is widely recognized.

Harvard has a successful, long-term alumni group. By contrast, the Georgia Special Olympics started from a standing stop. A lot of the families with children in the program are not wealthy.

The question, then, is how you get the long-term funding for such programs. How do you build an endowment so that such groups will be here generations from now? You do it by attracting the people who can contribute financially to your mission.

A MATTER OF STEWARDSHIP

Although I had no personal experience in dealing with people with mental disabilities, I knew others who faced those challenges in their families. Once I saw what the Special Olympics was doing and how it was working in people's lives, I got involved. I think there are a lot of people like me, who are attracted to missions simply because they are inherently worthwhile. The number-one goal of any charity, in my view, is to make sure it is worthy of the gift, what it is doing makes a donor feel good about contributing money, and there is a good return on the charitable investment

That's what propels charitable giving. That's what keeps it alive. Whenever givers have the feeling that something is amiss, their funding can dry up. A charity has a responsibility to do right with the blessings that are poured upon it.

It is a stewardship issue, and there is plenty of evidence that some do not live up to that responsibility. Almost weekly, you can pick up the paper and read about mismanaged money that has been sidetracked from where it could do the most good.

What's going to compel people to support an organization when they see it is falling apart?

Great legacies can crumble that way. It happens, and it makes donors skeptical. That's part of the challenge. There are a lot of great institutions that have recruited great staff, and yet, poor decisions by a few people can cause great harm. If you think of the negative publicity that was directed toward Pennsylvania State University in recent years, you will see my point clearly.

Worthy causes attract money. If a cause is perceived as less than worthy, it will attract less money. It comes down to that.

CONCERNS OF THE HEART

The pages ahead will not be loaded with highly technical details about trusts and other financial tools and how to set them up. There are a lot of places where you can learn those things. In this book, I will be focusing on matters of the heart.

When most advisors engage clients in charitable planning, they focus on just the financial dimension of it. There is also the social dimension and the personal dimension. We all have money we know we will not keep, but instead of viewing that as an expense, why not capture it as an asset? What you do for society is part of your worth and, ultimately, part of your legacy.

And there's the personal aspect: What's important about money to you? When I ask people that question, they usually say something along the lines of "Well, money is important, but it is not the most important thing." They mention things such as health and family as having greater priority.

As Barbara Bush said, "At the end of your life, you will never regret not having passed one more test, not winning one more verdict or closing one more deal. You will regret time not spent with a husband, a friend, or a parent."

And so we are talking about something much larger than the financial dimension. Our social and personal dimensions embrace so much more. We live in a world where we have personal relationships, and we live in a social environment where it matters immensely how we interact with others.

I want to free you from the burden of thinking that charitable giving is impossible for you. You will find out in the pages ahead that you do indeed have what it takes to make an impact. My goal is to inspire you and to reassure you, not to provide you with a technical manual. You can learn those steps from many sources, but inspiration is another matter entirely. I want you to see why you should—and how you certainly could—do more regardless of your station in life.

A MENTALITY OF ABUNDANCE

Some people live with a mentality of scarcity and some with a mentality of abundance. Some think of charitable giving as taking a piece from their pie and giving it away so less pie remains for them and their family. But charitable giving is more like inflating a balloon. If you do this right, with the help of expert guidance, you can expand what's available for everyone.

The *why* precedes the *how*, and the *why* is more important. Advisors are full of the *how*. They can show you all sorts of techniques. I think the more important question is the *why*. What is the reason that charitable giving makes sense to begin with?

Any single reason would be right or wrong, depending on who you are and your experiences and what you hold dear to your heart. Until an advisor truly understands what you value, it will be hard for that person to effectively determine the best course of action for you. Once you know why, it becomes clearer how to do it.

Years ago I had a client who sold his business when he was still in his 40s. I had gotten him involved in the Special Olympics, and he involved his company too. A lot of his employees became active, and they loved it. He became one of the Special Olympics' lead sponsors. He sponsored an Atlanta Braves night for the organization. Hundreds of his employees volunteered.

When he sold his business, he called me. "I need you to help me with what to do with the rest of my life," he said. "I am coming into a bunch of money." We did some extensive financial planning and developed an analysis, and I invited him and his wife into the office to talk over our findings. We sat down in the conference room, and I started to open a big three-ring binder.

"Now, just what are we going to do today?" he asked.

"Well, I have all this information I need to present to you," I explained.

"No, you don't," he said. "We've talked many times, and I don't doubt that you know what you're doing. I just want to know what I need to do next. I don't want to go through that big book."

And so I gave him the steps, where he should wire money, when he and his wife should be examined for life insurance, and how to set up a couple of trusts.

"Fine," he said. "How about getting all that set up and done and just send me a bill? This meeting is over. That's what I hired you to do." That could never have worked out so smoothly if we had not spent the time on the *why*. He had gotten to the point of assuming that the *how* was just detail. He was a business person. That's the way he ran his life. He made the big decisions, and other people implemented them.

To many people, all those details can be daunting. They could spend the many hours required to educate themselves, but they do not have the time or inclination. They really do not want to know the details. They want to trust someone to handle them and make the best decisions on their behalf. And that trust begins to form when someone cares enough to look into the heart of the matter: the *why*.

HOW THE WORLD SHOULD WORK

It all starts with compassion. One of my clients is the widow of the former executive director of the Special Olympics program here in Georgia. He once told me about an incident he witnessed at one of the summer track events. Three of the children were in a race and rounding a turn when one of them fell. The other two stopped, turned around, picked him up, dusted him off, and only then, when they knew he was all right, did they continue the race.

"That's the way the world should work," he told me. That story of selfless concern, even during the heat of competition, is a lesson for all of us on how we should continue the race. We get to the point where we understand that we must do more than just look out for ourselves. "Let me win, but if I cannot win, let me be brave in the attempt" is the Special Olympics' motto. It's on a plaque that I keep in my office.

Those special athletes instinctively knew the principle of all for one. Think of the times when others have rallied on your behalf or helped to shape you into who you are today. Each of us can reach out in the spirit of one for all.

CHAPTER 1

SHARING OUR STORIES

In the classical age, when Greek and Roman society flourished in such cultural centers as Athens and Constantinople, community building was paramount. Those cultures placed a premium on intellectual and artistic development. The Greeks advanced a holistic sense of personal development that included body, mind, and spirit. They understood the beauty of a balanced life.

They also attended to matters of posterity. Plato, for example, bequeathed to his students the gardens where he had posed the philosophies that intrigue scholars to this day. It was a gift that lasted hundreds of years until Emperor Justinian shut it down during the Holy Roman Empire because it had been a pagan institution.

It was an early example of a legacy, which was not uncommon in classical culture. Such sentiments also flourished in the Renaissance, along with the arts and sciences. The people of Florence called Lorenzo de Medici Il Magnifico. He sponsored many of the famous art projects of the Florentine Renaissance, and he was a driving force behind artistic, humanistic, and civic policy. Notably, he was a sponsor of Michelangelo. Modern society could use such inspiration and motivation.

CIVIC-MINDED LEADERSHIP

The rise and fall of nations is largely a result of the direction and agenda established by the leadership. I think of my city of Atlanta, Georgia, today. It did not suffer the destruction that some communities experienced after the assassination of Rev. Dr. Martin Luther King, who was a native of the city. "That's not going to happen here," said the business and civic leaders of the time, and from that attitude arose the motto, "A city too busy to hate." Yes, we have our issues. But we are an example of how leadership can influence communities in a very positive way.

I find that people who are in the real estate development business are very civic minded. "Well, that makes sense for them," you might say, "because if you develop a nice place to live and work, that attracts more people. That's good for their business." True, but it is also beneficial to the community at large.

Benefactors underwrite the arts, the civic life, and the spiritual life of our communities, and nobody could fairly say that all of that is just for their personal gain. They view it as a civic investment. They see it as something larger they are doing to improve the world around them. We have that mindset in our society. I just wish we had more of it.

In communities and cultures throughout history, there always has been an element of poverty, which has been a fundamental concern of humanity through the ages. It is only when a society feels confident that its basic needs are being met that the arts and sciences can flourish. The leadership sets the pace, and when the population as a whole does not need to spend its energies seeking food and shelter and the basics of life, it will feel the freedom to pursue a higher purpose. Society reaches greater heights when individuals gain a sense of bounty and a motivation to share.

Think of a gray and bleak city that you have passed through, where the storefronts are shuttered and the people seem to shuffle along in the hope of just getting by, day to day. If the pall hanging over such a community struck you that way, imagine how it affects the spirit of those who live and work there. Contrast that to the beauty and vibrancy of other cities, places of great architecture that embrace aesthetics. In such communities, just walking down the street elevates the soul.

Inspiration, however, can arise in a slum or on an avenue of the arts. Those who have come to know they have more than enough of life's resources and who recognize they are part of a bigger plan will want to contribute. They may not feel they can save the world, but they believe they can do something, in some way, to make their community better.

When we feel that sense of fullness, we adopt the perspective of serving the greater good. It is giving back with the purpose of elevating the standard of living, quality of life. We want to give others a chance to have what we have. If we've had the privilege and honor of attaining an education or visiting museums or even just living in a decent home, we may want to do what we can to give others such opportunities.

Museums, churches, and many nonprofit charitable organizations have outreach programs. They serve those who do not reach out on their own, whether because of financial poverty, poverty of spirit, or poverty of knowledge. There is no lack of need, and such organizations, given sufficient financial capabilities, can lift the whole population. In that spirit, civic minded leadership strives for the betterment of our communities. That is where we find the attitude of "that's not going to happen here," or "we can turn this around."

MY ROOTS IN GREECE

I do not pretend to be a Plato, but I do have a connection with Greece. I spent the first ten years of my life there.

My father grew up on a farm in western Maryland. He was one of 13 brothers and sisters, and he was the only one of his brothers to leave the farm. Several of his sisters left, but all of his brothers stayed and continued farming. One day my father flagged down the milk train that went through their little community. He went to Washington DC, where he got a job and lived in a boarding house. Those were the days of the "free lunch and the nickel beer." He went to night school to study accounting.

With the coming of World War I, he joined the US Marine Corps. As a marine, he was based in Washington during the war, and he stayed there after the war until he went to work for a while at the Pennsylvania Railroad company, as an accountant.

In 1922 he had an opportunity to go to Greece as part of the post-war humanitarian efforts of the American Relief Administration, which was headed by the future president, Herbert Hoover. A buddy had told my father about this opportunity, and being young and unmarried and an adventurous fellow at heart, he decided to do it. He got a job in Greece with the American Red Cross, auditing the supplies that were being distributed to refugees of the Greco-Turkish war.

It was the first time my dad had been out of the country, and really it was the first time he had traveled that far from where he grew up, other than going to Parris Island for US Marine Corps training. He looked around Europe for a little bit and fell in love with the idea of living overseas. He saw Paris, Vienna, Prague, and Budapest. I do not know exactly how he ran into the people at R. J. Reynolds Tobacco Company, but they offered him a job. They needed someone with his ability.

He would have a 40-year career with R. J. Reynolds, all of it in Greece, except during the Second World War, when he had to come back to the United States because Greece fell to the Germans. Mussolini could not get it done, so Hitler came down to help him. My father worked his way into management at R. J. Reynolds and eventually became COO of the subsidiary, overseeing the whole operation in Greece and Turkey.

He eventually learned to speak, read, and write a little bit of Greek. When he met my mother, she was living in Izmir, Turkey. She was from a French and Greek family that had settled there in the import/export business. They met on a blind date during the war, while he was waiting to get back into Greece. They married, and once the Nazis were out, my father moved back to Greece with his bride. They settled in tobacco country in a small town on the northern coast, about eight miles from the ancient town of Philippi.

I was born in Frederick, Maryland, the reason being the civil war in Greece at the time. After the Second World War, the Communists came into Greece. It was unknown whether they would take over or not, but there was gunfire in our town, and my mother was about to give birth to me. So my father sent her to live with his relatives in western Maryland. Talk about a cultural shock; my mother did not speak English well. Three months after I was born, he came for us, and we went back, although my mother had obtained her American citizenship. That was 1947, and I lived in Greece for the next ten years.

<u>STROLLING UPON ANTIQUITY</u>

In that post-war era, Greeks loved Americans. My father had a good, even prestigious job because he was viewed as someone who had helped to bring economic prosperity to the country. He bought tobacco and shipped it to the United States, enriching the local economy. A number of Greeks who did business with my father did very well economically.

Americans were viewed favorably because they had saved the world from fascism. That attitude continued until the 1960s. I went back to Greece with my dad, just the two of us, in 1965, during my summer between high school and college. By that time, he had been retired for four years, and he got to see his old buddies.

"Dad, I want to do what you did," I recall telling him during the trip.

"No, you don't," he said. "It is changed here now, and it is going to change even more. You need to find something else to do."

Growing up, I was homeschooled; there was no English-speaking school nearby. I had a tutor, Miss Helen, who was Greek but spoke beautiful English. She worked out the curriculum for me through a correspondence program known as the Calvert School. It was a structured course with tests and proficiency requirements that I went through for several years.

As a child, I learned to speak Greek and also French, the language of my mother's family. I spoke French when we visited my cousins, which was frequently, especially in the summers. I still have family in Greece and Turkey on my mother's side. We keep in touch and visit, and one of my nephews came to the United States for educational and career opportunities.

When I was ten, my father decided he wanted me to go back to the United States so that I might better understand and appreciate who I was and the fact that I was an American. When my dad said it was time for me to leave Greece, it was traumatic. I did not want to go.

You can imagine. We had a wonderful life. We lived well. I had no brothers or sisters, but I had lots of friends, Greek friends. And I was told, "You're going to go halfway around the world, and we're going to put you in a military boarding school, and you will love it."

Once I got here, I did love it—for the first year and for the second year too. But by the third year, I had decided it was not for me. All in all, however, the experience was fine. There were two types of kids in boarding school: brats and those whose parents were abroad. I was in the latter category. My father had considered sending me to school in England at first, but England was not his style. He wanted me to be an all-American boy. He wanted me to be play baseball, not cricket.

My father retired when he turned 65 and returned to the United States. I was only 14. My father married later than most men. A couple of years before his retirement, he bought a house, and one of his sisters stayed in it. Then, my mother came over to live there too, and it made a lot more sense for me to live at home than at the boarding school. And so I went to a local Catholic parochial school, and by the time my dad joined us, I was ready for high school in Baltimore.

We were all together again, and I would continue to grow up as an American boy. But I think often of my boyhood near Phillipi, where Aristotle once tutored Alexander the Great and where the disciples Paul and Silas were imprisoned. I was touched by the community's historic and spiritual significance. I was strolling upon antiquity.

It was a privilege to spend those years there. I did not fully realize it at the time, but I certainly have felt that way whenever I have gone back. Standing at the edge of the Aegean Sea, you can look out and imagine what took place on those waters and on those shores a lifetime or many lifetimes ago.

THE POWER OF RELATIONSHIPS

We need to feel free to tell one another our stories, for in that way, we express the elements of human connection that each of us has within us. When people are able to share their stories and communicate on that level, they relax. If the chemistry is not there, it will not work. But once we find out about one another, we forge the bonds of enduring relationships.

Through such personal communication I find I get a sense of the other individual's worldview. I pick up on how others generally feel about things. I think we all have a tendency to help people try to solve problems and to give advice, and by listening intently, we can learn what they truly want and need.

A lot of people have stories that are not as pleasant as mine. They have overcome circumstances with admirable character, and their experiences helped to build that character. I have not had a perfect life, but I'll tell you I would not trade any of it, neither the highs nor the lows.

You find out a lot about people when they talk about their journey and their families. In my business, people tell you everything. I often wish I had taken more psychology courses in college because people pour their hearts out when you talk to them about their money.

As I mentioned before, you deal better with people who are more like you. You can communicate in a sort of shorthand. However, one must be open to others. I have clients across the political spectrum. I have relationships across a variety of philosophical dimensions.

Having such diverse connections shows you can get along with a variety of folks. For all our sakes, we need to open up and talk to one another about ourselves. We need to share what is important to each of us.

Many financial advisors tend to short-circuit the client-advisor relationship and go right to the solution. I cannot do that. You can't really work with someone at arm's length. Clients need a trusted partner who understands what is important. They need an advisor who can walk in their shoes.

Each of us needs to find a greater purpose. Helping people tap into their philanthropic desires is fulfilling to me. It is more than a business to me. It is a responsibility that I take to heart.

When I see what my job accomplishes, I do not go home tired after a long day.

I have shared with you stories from my past because I know that you too have a story inside you. Each of us has one. Each of us has a place that we called home, sometimes far away, and I never tire of hearing those tales. I have found that clients who are eager to tell their stories, particularly when they involve themes of gratitude, are also inclined to think charitably.

I recently met the development director of a charity here in town. She attended one of my "Lunch and Learn" events, which I hold quarterly to provide updates to the nonprofit community regarding the challenges and opportunities they face in planned giving. At a follow-up session, I asked her, "Well, what did you think about what you heard when you came to lunch?"

"Oh, I loved it," she said. "You're so approachable."

That's a good word. I like that word. I am past the point of trying to impress people with what I know. But I do want them to feel at ease when talking with me. When they feel that level of comfort, I know I have connected.

CUTTING MY TEETH

I was first exposed to the field of financial planning while I was in graduate school at Loyola University in Baltimore, after receiving my undergraduate degree at Villanova, near Philadelphia. My major at both schools was in business administration.

It started to dawn on me that there was an area of investing out there that was broader than just the focus on stocks and bonds. It involved people's life goals and objectives and the meat and potatoes of why and how they invested, beyond the mechanics of investing. People had needs. Not only did they have to live from day to day but they wanted to educate their children and would, at some point, want to retire. The head of a household would want to make provisions for the family to survive and do well, come what may.

During my graduate school years and right afterward, my first job was with a life insurance company in New England. One of my college roommates had married into a wealthy family that lived in New York. My wife and I were living in Hartford, Connecticut, so we would visit them.

That family had a staff of attorneys, accountants, investment advisors, tax experts, and people knowledgeable about private equity. The team was just for that one family, which had been served that way for several generations. I thought how cool it would be if everyone, not just wealthy people, could have those kinds of connections. At the time, that was not the case. Most people dealt with a broker or insurance agent or lawyer, who often worked at cross purposes. They weren't working with a team.

The profession of financial planning has evolved over the years. As a matter of fact, this particular group, called the Bessemer Trust, has taken that team concept and marketed it outside the family to a lot of other people. I take that approach too but in a boutique environment rather than the big, New York skyscraper environment.

At the time, a life insurance agent would tell you that life insurance was the solution to most of your financial problems. Same thing if you talked to a stockbroker or someone in the real estate investment business. They knew where their bread was buttered, so to speak.

My thought was that we could change the paradigm so the clients would be the ones in control and could say, "I need to get from point A to point B in my life, financially, so what's the best way, or the best ways, to do that?" And it would all be laid out for them. I saw that as the ideal.

The life insurance company where I worked had started some of that. It bought a Boston money manager. I developed financial plans for widows and for executives. We had several large Fortune 500 companies as clients. Those executives had complicated compensation packages with stock options and deferred compensation. They had a number of opportunities to come out pretty well, financially, by the time they retired.

That was a great way for me to cut my teeth in this personal financial planning area. I started doing the analysis work that led to the solutions. And, even though I worked for a life insurance company, many times, these were investment solutions. The fact that we had an investment firm was a great advantage. That experience was the beginning of a career I still engage in today, 40 years later.

A CHARITABLE EMPHASIS

Then, I ran into a group from Atlanta that was taking the concept to a higher level. It had the CPAs, attorneys, real estate specialists, and retirement plan specialists all on board to provide those services for clients. It was a smaller but cutting-edge operation when I came to Atlanta to join it.

Unfortunately, it did not handle its own finances very well. I and my future partners, who also worked at that company, decided, in 1974, to strike out on our own. For 25 years, we ran a company that replicated that team idea. We had a tax attorney on staff, and we merged with a small accounting firm, and we did the investments. We did all of it very successfully.

We are all still in Atlanta, though no longer together. As we got to a certain age and brought children into the business, we decided it would be better that we separate, which has all worked out just fine.

I did not pay much attention, at first, to the charitable aspect of the profession. It was part of what some people did but not everything they did. Then, several years ago, I took a look at my career during a reflective moment at year's end. I noticed one thing that most of my clients had in common: philanthropic planning, some of it very sophisticated, some of it very basic. Over the years, I had been active on charitable boards, chaired campaigns, and helped grow several endowments—all of that, pro bono. Charities certainly do not mind having financial people around. You are recruited to a lot of boards if you're working in the financial area. And I was very glad to do it. I could see the positive effects of the endowments we built, such as patching a school roof or starting a Hispanic ministry at a church.

I got a little more intentional about it, you might say. Today, I am recognized as one who can help both charity and donor improve their financial situation by aligning their interests.

FINDING ONE'S PURPOSE

Most people are not aware of what is possible. "Let me show you what's possible," I tell them. "You probably don't know." They tell me that lawyers and others have advised them for years about which steps they should take. But when I show them what else they could have done, they are surprised to learn about it.

Think of your own stories and the paths you have taken in your personal life and professional career. Think of the causes you have come to admire and the institutions that molded you and changed your course. I am dedicated to using my talents with finance to help people perpetuate these good causes. I have found my purpose.

You too will do well to discover your purpose. The quest will bring meaning and reason to your financial planning, and it will help you to identify the causes and the people you wish to support.

It comes down, again, to knowing the *why* so that you can do the right *what*. Once you know your purpose, you can figure out the strategies to advance it. You attain a sense of clarity and confidence. The *why* is what steers the ship. You figure out what's important.

When you are clear about what matters most to you, it becomes a barometer for your decisions. You ask yourself, "Why am I doing this?" You answer, "Well, because it makes sense when I think about what I want to do with my life."

CHAPTER 2

WHAT'S IT ALL ABOUT?

I met someone at the airport as each of us was returning to Atlanta from spring break in Jamaica. I knew him because our children went to school together. I was on the board of that school and had chaired its capital campaign, and he was a contributor. We began to chat, and he mentioned to me that he needed to come in to talk to me about a project he had been setting up.

He owned a farm where he was operating a charity for inner-city kids. Most of them were delinquent kids who had been in trouble of one sort or another. He had developed what is called an operating charity. He had employees and a structured program to take those children out of their urban environment to spend time on the farm during the summer months, learning skills in a new setting.

I found his endeavor to be fascinating. He had contacted some state agencies so they could check him out to make sure they could support the activities on his farm. They would also help identify which children would be given the opportunity to spend time at the farm.

He became my client and had a successful business career, which, again, I have found to be the case with a lot of people who are similarly motivated to reach out to help others. He wanted to give young people an opportunity that they might not ordinarily have had. He dedicated himself to doing what he could to show them that the world was not the lousy place they might have come to think it was.

I was privileged to do what I could to advance his project. His ambition was to develop a template. He wanted to attract other entrepreneurs like himself, who would offer such opportunities to children in other communities.

WHERE WILL YOU LEAVE YOUR PRINTS?

Typically, when I start a discussion with people about money, we get to this issue of legacy. We begin to talk about the people, causes, and institutions that mean the most to them.

They often think first of family. To have an influence on our loved ones is a primal and noble ambition. But beyond that, they think of the causes they care about, the political affiliations and social movements they support. And they think about the institutions that have meant so much to them. Most of the people with whom I deal professionally have come to feel some such attachment. Perhaps, they see how much their education has benefited them, or if they are religious, they often deeply value the spiritual influence their relationship with a church or synagogue or other place of worship has had on their lives.

Their bonds with such causes and institutions tend to transcend personalities. They see beyond the immediate issues, for the most part, and understand that the institution or the movement itself is most important to them. Or if their focus is on family, they will look for ways to do something that generations hence will find meaningful. And it is not just about money. Many people desire to pass on values and knowledge garnered over a lifetime. They become mentors and role models. They strive to live their lives as an inspiration to others to look closely at how they are living their own.

When I introduce this concept to potential donors during presentations, I hold up a water glass. I tell them that if someone wanted to track me down, he could take my fingerprints off that glass. "But let's talk about it in positive terms," I say. "During your lifetime, what can you leave your mark on so that it will be there when you are gone?" We call that your "life print."

Really, to leave your mark is a human instinct—the one that yearns to declare, "I was here." From the depths of the heart, each of us wants to say, "I was here. I did something."

Some people want to be remembered for generations to come. They want to pass on their values. They ask themselves, as they get older, "How will I be regarded? How will people remember me? In two or three generations, will they remember me at all?"

A WEALTH OF DREAMS

When most people talk about what money means to them and what is important about it, they begin to discuss the legacy part of it, the life prints. They also talk about dreams, asserting that they would do this thing or that if only they had enough money. When I ask people, "What is wealth? What does wealth mean to you?" their first response tends not to be about money. People talk about family. They talk about health. They talk about being self-contained and self-satisfied.

Money is in there. It is certainly among the top five answers people give to my question. But rarely is it at the top. Money, after all, is just a tool for accomplishing other things. You have to put it in its proper place.

Bob Buford is a successful Texan who did well in the cable business. He had a long-term relationship with Peter Drucker, the preeminent management guru who died recently at 91, and he has led an effort to preserve and advance Drucker's philosophies for future business and nonprofit leaders. Buford sold his business and was looking around for what to do with the rest of his life. He developed the concept of "moving from success to significance" and wrote the book *Halftime* on that theme.

There are a lot of people like that. They do not necessarily have to sell their business, but they're at a stage of life where their business, or their profession, is not all-consuming anymore. They have some skills and interests outside their primary vocation and find themselves pondering how they might spend their time doing something of significance.

Their vision is to leave the community a better place. That may well have been a long-term desire, but now they have gained both the financial resources and the time, and they still have the energy to make things happen.

I was playing golf with a man who had recently started his retirement. "How do you like it?" I asked.

"Well, it's great to have time for things," he said. "I get to see the kids and grandkids when I want. I finally can do some things I've always wanted to do," and he told me about the charities with which he had become involved. "I'm having the time of my life."

Today, if you retire in your mid-60s to mid-70s, you may have quite a bit of time ahead of you because of the advances in medicine and the fact that many of us take better care of ourselves than, perhaps, our parents did.

HOW MUCH TO THE KIDS?

Your contributions need not be at the societal level. They can be very localized: the community or the family. As we'll see in upcoming chapters, a major concern that people have is whether they will rob their family if they leave money to charity.

I receive *Investment News*, a weekly periodical. A recent article was titled "Sting Joins Chorus of Wealthy Who Will Not Leave Fortunes to Kids."[1] He wanted his children to know where he stood. The tone of the article was that he didn't want to leave them a trust fund out of concern that they wouldn't do anything of value with their lives.

Instead, you can help the next generation develop money skills by demonstrating philanthropy to them. They can learn about causes that are worthy of support. They can learn how that money can be managed so it lasts. Those are valuable lessons—and philanthropy isn't just for the very wealthy. The average person can join that conversation.

Most people, in their desire to be viewed as significant, aren't thinking it should all be in the eyes of their children. If they have excess money, they don't necessarily believe it should all go to their children. They have other destinations for their legacy.

However, this need not be a Sophie's choice of one or the other. The money can go to the kids in a tax-efficient manner and benefit the family while also benefiting charity. It is not as if a decision to become significant to society means we need to exclude our children.

Still, we can determine how much might be helpful to them and how much could be harmful. That might be different for each child. Some would use an inheritance wisely, and others would

---

1 *Investment News* article by Liz Skinner, June 23, 2014.

use it foolishly, even to their own detriment. Such matters lead to major discussions, reflecting the depth of people's concerns.

WHERE THERE'S A WAY, THERE'S A WILL

When I speak at events or even when I'm just out and about, I can sense when people are interested in what I do and want to talk to me. I see them lingering, considering how to broach the subject. They're curious and want to know more. They will take me aside for a chat, or a friend or colleague will introduce me to them.

Such conversations typically begin with some concern they have. They all want to know whether they have enough money. Are they going to run out? I often give them examples of things they could do and options that are available to them. "Do you know," I might say, "that you can increase your income and lower your taxes and benefit the causes you care about?"

I am seen more and more as a specialist on this topic of philanthropy. Because of my involvement on boards and the sort of pro bono work I've done, people have seen what I have helped others to do and want to learn how they too might apply these strategies.

Something inside them makes them want to do more. They are curious whether there might be a way to do it that they haven't heard about. Once they feel that spark and get answers to a few basic questions, the possibilities blossom. The conversation can develop in many ways, and I certainly can reassure people that, yes, they can do this.

Many years ago, my neighbors came into the office. The husband was a corporate officer for a large company. The couple would retire comfortably, though not extravagantly. They wanted to buy a vacation property and could not figure out how to do it. We did some analysis that indicated they could afford the property, which they still have today, 15 years later. Soon, their friends were calling, asking how they might afford a vacation property too.

The point is that people are often not aware of the possibilities. If they can find a trustworthy source to show them how to do things without taking on a lot of risk and jeopardizing their finances, they will take action and may accomplish much, whether charitable in nature or otherwise.

CHAPTER 3

LIFE'S NEXT STEPS

Let me tell you a story about a Swedish chemist who discovered a system for producing dynamite. He became very successful, with manufacturing facilities around the world. One day his brother died, but the papers made a mistake. They thought it was the chemist who had died, and they published his name and life story in the obituary section.

He did not like what he read. The newspapers said that as the inventor of dynamite, he would be remembered as an author of war and destruction. They called him a "merchant of death."

He had hoped he had invented something with such power that a war would be too horrible to contemplate and his invention would end all wars. "I'm going to do something about this," he vowed. "I'm going to change the course of my life."

He had a different vision of himself than others had. They saw him as a warmonger. He saw himself as a peacemaker.

The Swedish chemist's name was Alfred Nobel, a name and reputation without need of further explanation. The message here is that it is never too late.

FROM DREAM TO REALITY

Nobel had a great awakening that produced a significant result. To read one's own obituary is an opportunity not likely to befall many people, but our eyes open in many other ways, and we recognize that if we want to be remembered for the dreams we had, we need to do something concrete to make them happen.

It was once explained to me that after you write down an idea, the brain begins to process it differently. What had been floating freely is now taking anchor. When you commit that idea to paper, it becomes palpable. It feels more real. It no longer feels like daydreaming. It feels like a goal and you feel motivated to look for solutions to advance that goal.

We've had a number of clients who received early retirement offers making them feel that retirement was coming out of the blue. They did not have a plan for how it might work, and so they came to us to help them figure out whether they should take this step. We sat down and developed a spending plan for possible retirement that covered the nuts and bolts, the practical matters, along with considerations such as how much they could travel. A lot of those people have now been retired for five to ten years. We monitor their situation every six months to see how they are doing.

In other words, we have worked with them to get it all down on paper—and on the computer screen. Retirement has turned from a vague dream into a goal that is being accomplished.

It is a stressful time, particularly when the opportunity comes earlier than expected. How can you go from living on one salary or two salaries to living on no salary, just one, relatively limited pot of money? What's the risk? If the market goes down, as it did in 2008, what are the consequences? We can model all of those considerations and advise you that either yes, you can, or no, you cannot. We can tell you the maximum you can spend each year and explain other parameters.

We monitor the plan every six months so the client can make adjustments, if necessary, to stay on track. Some expenses might not be anticipated. For example, if a son loses his job, the parents may support him for a few months. We take that into account, as well as whether the son pays them back after he finds a new job.

We encounter situations such as that every day. The monitoring and adjusting need to continue into retirement. In their financial planning, people face such uncertainties as income level and the costs of housing or medical care. Given the changes in their lives, they need to know how long the assets will last.

Again, that can all be anticipated and estimated and put down on paper, with adjustments going forward. It's the fear of what they can't see coming that will keep people up at night.

THE PROPER ORDER OF THINGS

Most advisors focus on what they think you should do. They tell you to make certain moves, do certain things to make other things happen. Instead, I think you have to back up and start by asking yourself what you want to do.

That's when the genie comes out of the bottle. People say many things as they reveal their dreams and worries and strategies:

"Well, I want to be sure I do not go broke."

"I want to be sure I have $100,000 dollars a year of income."

"I want to be sure the children will get this, this, and this."

"I want my money to go to benefit society through the institutions I choose, not just go to taxes."

"I want to travel to Paris and Amsterdam."

"I want to be able to spend plenty of time with the grandkids."

They want the Norman Rockwell painting, generally. They want the ideal. "Okay, fine," I say, "that's what you want to do. What do you have?"

"Well, I have all these assets, a retirement plan, a house. I have money here and there. I have investments. I have a business."

"Okay, good. Now we can develop what you should do."

That's the proper order, in my view. The advice on the Internet and the rest of the media is general in nature. It really couldn't be otherwise. It's like general medical advice, which can be sensible but in no way takes the individual into consideration. "Eat right, and exercise." Yes, but eating right for me might not be the same for you. Vigorous exercise could benefit one person but could kill another.

Similarly, in financial planning and wealth management, you first need to consider your individual circumstances and what you want to accomplish. You still will be buying groceries and maintaining a certain lifestyle and may want to take a couple of trips each year. In other words, you have needs and you have wants, and the costs of each can be calculated.

Then, you look at your assets and figure out what you have to do to meet those costs. And along the way, I often ask this question: "If I could show you a tax-efficient way to do this that would benefit you, your children, and charity, would that be something you would want to look into?

"Oh, I would love that. That would be great."

People must identify their needs and wants first. Once you break needs and wants down, the solution gets easier because needs and wants are just price tags. My lifestyle is a price tag. It takes so much each year. Some of those expenses are needs: the mortgage and utilities, the groceries and gas. Some are wants: the family cruise.

When you can see the price tag, you can make a decision on what you can afford. How much money will you have coming in and from where? Social Security? A pension? What else? You need to determine whether the income covers your needs and wants. Maybe you can fund them all, but if not, you must prioritize and adjust your expectations. Maybe you just spend $50,000 on a wedding and not $100,000. Maybe you treat the family to a less extravagant vacation, or maybe you find a way to arrange your finances to produce more income or reduce your current taxes.

Seeing it all quantified is what gives people the clarity and confidence to act. Before moving forward, they're looking for any gaps. They want to make sure they've got it all covered: the fundamental needs, the contingencies, and the finer things they want in life. First, they should budget their needs and then their wants—and the latter, if need be, can be scaled down or skipped.

After that comes the vision. Once people see that they're secure and that their own interests are satisfied, they are able to turn their thoughts toward reaching out. They should write down those aspirations as well. Remember the power of putting it on paper. And then, looking backward, they can determine whether they are on track with how they imagined life would be.

WRITING YOUR OWN EULOGY

Imagine yourself, like Alfred Nobel, reading your own obituary. Would you like what you see? Try writing your own eulogy as you would desire it to be. What meant the most to you? What made you sad? What made you angry? What brought you joy?

I am not saying you need to be shocked into action. Most people, as they age, naturally begin to think long thoughts about the meaning of their lives and how they have touched others. When you're young and having fun and advancing in your career, you're not thinking so much about the *why* of your existence. Sometimes you're thinking about the *how* of your existence, as in how you will get through this particular day.

You have a whole different mindset as you get older, and that's why you need thorough financial planning more than ever. In this chapter, we have talked about the basics: the needs, the wants, and the vision and putting those things in the right order. The next chapter will go into the financial planning process in more detail.

CHAPTER 4

DO YOU HAVE ENOUGH?

"For many of us, the great obstacle to charity lies not in our luxurious living or desire for more money, but in our fear—fear of insecurity."
—C. S. Lewis

S am, a high-powered executive, had a heart for charitable giving. I once attended a banquet where he was given an award for all he had done to reach out to help others and for his faithful service as a board member.

As I watched Sam accept that much-deserved award, I could not help but think he could have done so much more. He was a client of mine who had decided to wait a little longer before taking my advice regarding his personal finances. He waited too long, and now, there was not much he could do.

As he neared retirement, he had one stock that was worth $6 million, acquired through options over the years with his company. He also had a million dollars coming from an inheritance.

I had recommended that his stock go immediately into a charitable trust, where it could be sold without incurring a capital gains tax. He would get an income of 5 percent a year, and he would keep control over where the money eventually went.

But he waited, expecting a year of great earnings. The stock was at $80 a share. Two years later, it was at $6 a share.

If Sam had put stock into the trust, it could have been sold without incurring any capital gains tax, and he could have gotten an income of 5 percent a year from the trust for as long as he lived. That's an important point because the stock, at the time, paid a minimal dividend of only about 1 percent. On top of that, he would have received a substantial current-year income tax deduction.

He was looking at some great advantages. He wouldn't be paying the capital gains, he would have more income for the rest of his life, he would get a tax deduction, and he would get to diversify the portfolio, which reduces risk. If there's any free lunch in the world of investing, it is diversification.

But he waited. "Well, I know the company's doing great," he said. "Why don't we wait awhile? I think the stock will be worth even more." The stock, however, was about as high as it ever got when we had that conversation. It was a technology stock, and this was just before the tech bubble burst in 2000–2001.

THE CONSEQUENCES OF HESITATION

It is a story that happens time and time again, with many of those sad tales arising from the nightmare of 2007–2008. People hesitate to take action, and they—and society—lose so much.

I often suggest that people "put a toe in the water." Sam could have set aside, perhaps, half of that $6 million to see how things went. He had already accumulated enough to do great good, while improving his own situation, but he did not take action.

That kind of scenario is replayed every decade or so. In 2000, it was the tech bust. It was the financial companies and banks in 2008. It was real estate back in the mid-1970s and oil in the 1980s.

The year my father retired from R. J. Reynolds, the surgeon general came out with the report that linked cigarette smoking to lung cancer, and my dad had a great deal of his wealth tied up in R. J. Reynolds stock. He took a huge hit right at a crucial point in the family's financial life. We weren't thrown out on the street, but it took a long time for that situation to recover.

Any one company can be vulnerable to not only internal circumstances but external events as well. The way to get rich in this country is to have a concentrated position in a business that grows like crazy, but the way to stay rich is to diversify that position over time.

TRAPPED IN THE CYCLES

Sam thought he was being wise. He thought he saw a good thing getting better, but his assets were not diversified. His wealth was all in his company's holdings, and he paid the penalty for that, a huge one.

When people work at a company that's doing well, it is understandable that they do not feel vulnerable. But there are cycles in everything. There are cycles in the weather, in your health, in the stock market, in the economy, in interest rates—you name it. One of the keys is to recognize where you are at the moment. We may not have a crystal ball, but it's helpful to have a wind sock.

My thought, as I watched Sam at the banquet, was how much more he could have done had he taken advantage of what was available to him. He made significant contributions in time, talent, and treasure, but those contributions could have been so much greater. He could have benefited tremendously, and charity could have benefited tremendously. Instead of a win-win, his situation became a lose-lose.

There are far too many such sad tales that could be told. In just about every town in America many people have greatly benefited from some company and have pinned their dreams on those benefits. Times change. When I was in college, I labored at Bethlehem Steel in the summers. I was at the Sparrows Point plant in Baltimore. The property stretched for acres and acres and actually included employee housing. It was union work at union pay.

Where is Bethlehem Steel today? I recently met a financier who had bought the company out of bankruptcy, and I told him I once had worked there. He smiled. "I could have told you," I said, "what was going to happen to that company when I worked there."

You can take advantage of economic cycles, but too often, you get caught in them and trapped. Fortunes rise and fortunes fall, and that's why your hopes never should be pinned to one company, one enterprise. You need more than just one fountain for your dreams.

DISABLED BY FEARS

The lesson is that you cannot depend on any one investment for your future. From a risk management perspective, you have to look at diversifying your positions.

A lot of people are reluctant to diversify because of the big tax bill they would face. However, charitable planning gives you an opportunity to avoid that tax, get diversified, and even receive an income you cannot outlive, along with a current tax benefit. An individual can accomplish personal financial goals that will also benefit the charity. The only loser in the deal is the IRS. You can do this whether the asset is stocks, cash, real estate, a business, a farm, a house, or even artwork. It doesn't have to be worth multimillions. The gift can be large or small. It depends upon what the client wants to do.

So why do people hesitate? You would think they would want to make the most of what they have, and yet, they fail to take action. They and society lose so much. Why do they wait? If I knew the answer to that question, I would unlock the secrets to my profession. I think part of it is that most advisors and their clients only deal with the financial dimension. It needs to go beyond that to those social and personal dimensions that I mentioned earlier. People need to see the impact they could make. We're taking money that ordinarily the IRS would have gotten and transferring it to charity, to the causes and institutions that people care about. Meanwhile, the client benefits personally and financially in terms of tax deductions and maybe more income, more cash flow.

Fear and greed are great motivators, but neither of those emotions should hold sway during financial planning. Worry about the unknown certainly can paralyze. I often suggest that people put a toe in the water and do a trial run with part of their resources. That makes it less scary for them. Once they gain confidence, they will feel motivated to do even more good. The trick is not to wait too long, for whatever reason, including the hope of a market rally that allows you to accomplish even more. You well may end up only able to accomplish much less.

PUTTING IT TO THE STRESS TEST

Analytically, we can play what-if games. What if we went through another recession like 2008 and 2009? How would your financial plan endure, as it is currently configured, in that kind of economic climate? What if you never get Social Security benefits, as many young people today assume? What if the inflation rate were to increase? What if you took a big hit in the market or just had to endure years of sluggish returns? What if you invested mostly in bonds?

What if you require extended medical care? We can make some reasonable estimates based on your family history and your current health situation. How would that be funded? What if you or your spouse were to die?

We can model the effect that such circumstances would have. Do you have enough to get through them, or are there some gaps there? I enjoy golf. Golf instructors talk about power leaks in a swing that can prevent a golfer from bringing the most strength to the ball in the most efficient way at the moment of impact. Are there any power leaks in your financial plan? Are there some things you are not aware of that could blindside you?

Stress-testing has been a popular term in the financial vernacular ever since the banking crisis, when there was a lot of talk about stress-testing the banks to see how they would fare if certain things happened in the economy. We can do that for individuals. What would happen to your portfolio if certain conditions came about one at a time or simultaneously? What are the probabilities of these things occurring?

How in the world, you may be wondering, can anyone account for all of those variables? So many things can go wrong. I would answer by saying that the computer has been one of the great inventions of all time. Years ago we did this by hand. It was tedious. Today we have software. I agree it's part science and part art, but we can certainly change our assumptions very easily on the computer and we can see the results graphically and immediately. You can adjust for the inflation rate and see what effect that will have on your future spending.

When you're going to have to rely on your asset base, either entirely or in part, this exercise gives you a look at what you could be up against. You see how much cash flow you will have over your life expectancy, depending on your needs and wants. A new car every few years? A nice wedding for your daughter or granddaughter? We can model the scenarios. The computer quickly shows the ramifications.

So we first put together a picture of people's aspirations and goals for the future. Then, we put a price tag on those things and employ the power of the computer to see how the future would look. It is really not all that complex. You're either increasing or decreasing the amounts on those price tags.

The microchip has allowed us to do a great many things. We can simplify complex calculations and present them in under-standable form. That's where science meets art because, ultimately, the emphasis must be on human beings and what they want out of life and what matters most to them.

We all wonder if we have enough. One might presume that people with a lot of money would feel confident, but often, they are not. They have certain spending requirements and a lifestyle to which they are accustomed. They may be underwriting expenses for children or grandchildren. They too wonder whether their cash flow will see them through. In my career, maybe one or two people have told me, "I've got plenty. I'll never spend as much as I have." The rest haven't been so certain. They want reassurance, and stress-testing helps them find it.

The more money you have, the more the demands on your income and nest egg increase. If you have $10 million, you can feel as worried and stressed as someone living from hand to mouth. I see that over and over again. For some, that $10 million might seem to barely suffice, considering all the expectations and the goals.

You need not wonder. You can stress-test your financial situation for all the issues, including the final eventuality: what happens to the money when you are gone? Once you see that big picture, you can take steps to ease that stress. You can learn to do more with less. And you very well might see that you will have a surplus as the years go by. The question, then, is where does that surplus go? How should it be divvied up? That's when we can talk about the charitable strategies that will make the most of your wealth to the betterment of all involved.

MANAGING RISK

I am a big believer in avoiding unnecessary risk. Taking more risk than necessary to accomplish your aims is my definition of greed. If you can meet your needs and goals with conservative, guaranteed investments, that's what you should do first.

If it turns out that you could well be running out of money in 15 or 20 years, you could decide to go further out on the risk spectrum with investments that could bring in more gain. That strategy could work out, but a wise investor would look closely at its potential to backfire. You should look to preserve what you have before taking on an appropriate amount of risk, with the appropriate portion of your money to handle the wants of life, including the desire to benefit charity.

It is important to determine how much risk you are willing to accept. How much can your portfolio tolerate, and how much can you tolerate and still be able to get a good night's sleep? We can show, analytically, how much risk your portfolio can accept. But there's also that personal dimension. "I just couldn't live through another 2008," I hear people say. "I lost 40 percent!" That means we need to construct a portfolio that isn't subject to such risk, and if we do that, can we still meet their goals? We can run an analysis that answers yes, no, or maybe. We can compute the probabilities. If an economic event that only comes around every 30 years or so were to happen during your retirement, what would that do to your portfolio? And to your sense of well-being? In other words, can your portfolio handle it and can you?

WHAT THE TAX RETURN TELLS US

I have often said that if I could look at your checkbook and your calendar, I could tell you what's important to you. Where you spend your money and how you spend your time says everything. Your calendar and checkbook speak volumes about what is meaningful to you.

It's not that I would do such a thing. We're not looking to see how much you spend at the liquor store compared with what you're giving to your church. However, it is highly important that we review your tax return. It contains a wealth of information that will be valuable in helping you to chart your financial course. The return tells me, obviously, how much you pay in taxes. We often find missed opportunities due to missteps and miscalculations. People sometimes fail to take advantage of tax breaks that are built into the code. The return also shows me the extent of your investments and the amount of activity, and I can see your charitable interests.

A tax return functions for us in the way that an X-ray does for a doctor. It reveals a lot beneath the surface, and it points us in the right direction for further questions. You may have investments producing income that is all taxed, and we may be able to do something about that through some charitable planning. We might be able to reduce the tax on the investment income. From looking at the tax return, we can see your sources of income and whether they can be adjusted more favorably.

That tax examination is all part of the process of developing a thorough financial plan and identifying those needs, wants, and visions we discussed in the previous chapter. This is all part of finding out whether you have enough.

INCOME PLANNING

In setting up your investment priorities, you should allocate your money accordingly and in separate portfolio accounts. Think of those accounts as "buckets." Each bucket will be invested in accordance with how the money in it will be used. The sooner you will need the money, the less risk you can accept. You can accept somewhat more risk for money you will not need for several years. You can take even more risk on money not needed for many years or that you may leave to your heirs. The reason is that if the market corrects, long-term investments may have time to recover—*if* you aren't withdrawing income. You should only be using your conservatively invested short-term "bucket" for your spending income. The remainder of your money in those other buckets should go untouched for now.

The investments in a bucket can be made more conservative as you get closer to the time when the money will be spent. For example, a lot of parents and grandparents set up educational accounts for children when they're born. That amount can be subject to long-term investment risk. When those children reach 18 years of age, you'd better have that mostly in cash because you're going to need that money over the next four to six to eight years, depending on the educational timeframe. You do not want to subject it to risk. Not only do you want the money to be accessible and liquid, but you also want to avoid the prospect that it could vanish in the middle of your grandchild's sophomore year.

ATTAINING CLARITY

Once you have identified your needs, wants, and goals, and once you feel confident about your income and budget, you can look to see if anything is left over. You can set up the investment priorities for your money, keeping in mind the importance of preserving what you have gained.

If, in the end, charitable giving is included in the plan, that's fine. If charity is not included, that's okay too. What all this should produce is clarity about your personal situation and the confidence to act. In other words, you understand how you and others will benefit, and you are ready to make the necessary changes.

WHAT CAN TRULY HURT YOU

What you do not know can hurt you. An advisor knows not to assume that just because people have many millions, they're sophisticated in their financial thinking, and they have taken advantage of what's available.

People are often surprised when we tell them their documents do not reflect what they think is in them. The investments are not what they think, or a beneficiary designation is in dire need of updating. Somewhere along the line, things were done wrong or forgotten. I've seen wills and beneficiary designations on retirement plans that include spouses of divorced children.

I once reviewed the will of the chairman of a charitable board who was convinced that he had made a bequest to a particular organization. There were no charitable bequests. He had recently updated his will, and that got left out. He was dumbfounded. Something had fallen through the cracks, and that something could have meant a lifetime aspiration would not have been addressed. We fixed the issue right away.

This happens. Somebody doesn't push the right button when putting the documents together. We would never undertake an analysis of someone's situation without reviewing the original documents. It is just too risky to make an assumption based only on the client's perception of what has been done.

Often, for example, people have a will, beautifully drafted and executed. But all their assets are in their joint names, and because of that, those assets aren't addressed by the will. And if they have life insurance or retirement plans with beneficiary designations, a will does not apply, unless the beneficiary is the estate. This all calls for a periodic review to make sure such things are properly coordinated. We review wills annually. Without realizing it, in many cases, people make changes that affect the interplay of all of these assets.

Frankly, many people need to come to terms with the fact that they do not know everything, and that's okay. They probably gained their wealth through some talent other than financial savvy and investment skills. Each of us has a forte, and it well could be that the talent that created the money is not the same talent needed to hang on to it.

STEPS TO FINANCIAL SECURITY

Effective financial planning calls for ordering your steps, and people often get those steps out of sequence. They're not all that complicated, in their essence. Step one is "what do I want?" Step two is "what do I have?" Step three is "what should I do?"

Most advice is focused on "what should I do?", but you need to go through the first two steps before you can make a sensible decision on the third one. The first two determine the third.

You need to commit yourself to taking specific actions toward accomplishing the goals you have established. You should start today. There is an old saying: When is the best time to plant a tree? Twenty years ago. The second best time is today. Write down those goals and what is important to you. It is helpful to commit concepts, goals, and ideas to writing. You can go back to review your goals year after year, and perhaps, update them.

When seeking advice, hire a specialist. I heard that former Chief Justice Warren Burger wrote his own will instead of hiring a specialist, and, according to some accounts, his estate paid several hundred thousand dollars in unnecessary costs. You should get a written, integrated plan. By integrated, I mean financial decisions should never be made in a vacuum. You should know the effect of an investment change on your estate, or the effect of a gift on your income.

SOMEDAY, SOMEDAY...

People often say, "When I have more money, I will..." Does that describe you? If so, you are not alone. Many people give less than they truly want to give or than they should give. If you feel you have nothing to offer, you have been misled.

I am convinced that in my profession the two fundamental talents to master are questioning and storytelling. You need to be able to question without interrogating and still get the information you need. And you must ask the follow-up questions, similar to the way in which a doctor asks a patient whether he is sleeping well, feels stressed at work, or is eating a balanced diet. And people relate to stories. They do not remember statistics and factual information as well as they do stories about people experiencing things. That's how the mind grasps concepts and learns. It is why so many of the biblical lessons are parables.

Through attentive questioning and listening and effective storytelling, a good advisor can combat the negative voices in people's heads, the ones that are saying, "I do not know where to start, so why bother? This doesn't apply to me. This is for big people." I see what they often write on comment cards after I give a presentation: "Well, I think this is for people with a whole lot of money" or words to that effect.

You can have a lasting impact long after you are gone and still have a say on how your money will be used. I know from experience that people can do more, and they want to do more, once they are shown how they can do more.

CHAPTER 5

WILL YOU STILL HAVE ENOUGH?

Everybody knows Joe. He could be your neighbor. There's probably a Joe in your family who has done things similar to this particular gentleman.

Joe was 79 years old and a benefactor of a hospital in the Pittsburgh area. He attended one of our presentations that focus on donors. Afterward, he took advantage of our offer to consult with him to see if there was anything else he could do.

After that consultation, he transferred some of his wealth to a trust. As a result of that transfer, he was able to increase his current income by about 24 percent. He got a tax deduction for that year, and his trust was able to diversify and reduce his exposure to risk. He transferred stock, although what he accomplished can be done with many types of assets.

Not only was all of that very beneficial to him, personally, but the hospital benefited as well. The current tax deduction was money back in Joe's pocket, so he increased his donation to that institution. In the meantime, he also increased his annual giving because he was bringing in about one-fourth more in income. He now had the resources and felt the gratitude to give even more.

How did his income go up? After that portion of his wealth went into a charitable remainder trust, it was diversified. The trust now could pay out a higher income than he previously received from a stock paying a low dividend. He was able to increase his income as a result of the funds now being invested in higher-paying assets. And not a penny of gains tax was paid when the trust sold the original stock to reinvest.

However, if he had diversified that wealth outside the trust, he would have subjected that sale to tax that would have claimed upward of 20 percent of the value. It was not taxable within the trust because the charity eventually would get the proceeds upon his death.

When Joe found out about these techniques, he wanted to do even more. He changed his will to add a school, and then he added his church as a charity to his IRA.

Two years later, Joe died of a stroke. He was worth $3 million. As a result of what he had done, the hospital got about $900,000, and the other charities got $250,000 and $100,000.

And so, upon his death, the charities got about $1.3 million total. He had a son and a daughter. They came to us, and the daughter said, "We had no idea Dad was this charitably inclined. He gave away $1.3 million!"

We explained to them that as a result of that charitable planning, he benefited while he was alive: he got more income and a tax deduction. But aside from that, we explained, the family now benefited as well. Before the planning, we pointed out, nothing was going to charity, so the family was going to get $2 million and the Internal Revenue Service was going to get $1 million. We showed them that as a result of their father's planning, the brother and sister would now receive $2.6 million. Charity was now going to get $1.3 million, and the IRS was going to get zero.

"Yeah, but that's a lot of money going to charity," the daughter repeated, and so we went through the figures with them again. It amounted to convincing her that $2.6 million for the two of them was more than $2 million for the two of them. She finally understood that. She may not have been clear on the techniques that allowed it all to happen, but what mattered to all involved was really this: The charity was much better off. The family was much better off. The only loser in this arrangement was the IRS.

THE VOLUNTARY PHILANTHROPIST

That's the potential that is out there in this kind of work. Every case has potential. It may not be as dramatic as that one, but there's always something folks can do.

We changed Joe from being an involuntary philanthropist. He was about to give that million dollars to the IRS and not exactly willingly. Instead, he was able to take control and create an asset to benefit institutions that he cared about. He became a voluntary philanthropist.

When people ask why they should do this, I answer, "In terms of purely a return on investment, if you could choose whether to send a million dollars to the IRS or to charity, where would you invest? Where would you put your money? Where do you think the return would be best?" There is no doubt that charities generally deliver goods and services dramatically better than the tax system.

I am not saying that we should not have a tax system. We need to defend the country, and we need to have courts and police, for example. But there are many areas where charities can do such a much better job than the government in delivering resources and results. Most people intuitively feel that's the case, but no one has shown them how they might have a choice in directing where and how they contribute.

Joe's children saw that their father had taken the reins so that the money did not go to the IRS but, rather, to causes that he particularly valued and, at the same time, he had increased his legacy in terms of the resources he left to them.

MORE, NOT LESS

The bottom line is that charitable giving can leverage your money so that you can actually provide more, not less, for yourself and your loved ones. To help you make it happen, you need to work with a specialist who knows the possibilities and procedures. Most people do not know where to begin, and they are not going to learn it on the Internet.

First, they need to come to terms with the abundance, versus the scarcity, mentality. Some people operate on the assumption that there's only so much wealth; it is finite, and if someone else wins, they lose, and vice versa. That's just not true. We need to start with a mindset that rejects that way of thinking and asks, "How can I increase the abundance for all of us?"

It is an attitude of poverty to believe you are being cheated of your share if somebody else gets something. That attitude can exist even among the wealthy and those raised in affluence. Think about Ebenezer Scrooge, hoarding his money in his chambers before he was visited by the three spirits of Christmas.

The desire to give and make a difference is part of what makes us uniquely human, but so very often, people do much less than they could. I think most people have an innate desire to lead a life of significance and do something personally meaningful, but they haven't been shown how to use their money toward those ends. They may have been generous with their time and talents, but they do not yet understand how contributing money could mean more, not less, for them. This is not about writing a check and being done with it. This is about leveraging existing resources so that both donor and recipient are better off, financially.

People come to believe that they deserve the fruits of their years of hard work. That's not selfish. I'm not saying that you shouldn't take care of yourself, but stewardship means you are looking out not just for what is best for you but for what is best all around you. If you do something to contribute to a better society, that benefits you.

FOR THE BENEFIT OF ALL

People want to enjoy themselves. They want to live more. And they may very much want to give more. But they do not want to do one at the expense of the other, and the truth is they are not mutually exclusive. To me, the act of giving is part of living well. It makes us uniquely human.

I have a colleague who works for a historical preservation charity. He tells me that his best candidate for donations is the retired librarian who never married and has a home and an IRA. She has no heirs who will want her home when she dies. He gets people like her to consider donating their home. They can live in it until they die, and then the home goes to the charity.

The donor gets a current tax deduction for doing that, and even in the lowest tax bracket that deduction is worth something. She is now able to take more out of her IRA and not pay tax on it because she got the deduction for donating the house. That's a very simple tax scenario that could apply in a lot of places.

When people say, "I do not have enough," my answer always is "Let's see what you do have, and that will help us determine whether you have enough." People can make significant contributions without being a Rockefeller. If only big-name billionaires were to donate, would charities survive, particularly the smaller ones?

I have heard that in Memphis, at any given time, a couple of hundred wills are being probated, in which the St. Jude Children's Research Hospital is named as a beneficiary. The average gift is just a few thousand dollars. These are not large gifts, but the hospital is very good at securing them from people who feel grateful for what the institution has done.

Every charity would love a major gift. Here in Atlanta, the opera received $9 million from one of its board members who had died. It was a complete surprise to the institution, which had expected, at most, $1 million, and it was transformative for that organization. It had survived and now thrived with money for both endowment and operations. Everybody would love that kind of gift, and this example shows what potential already exists in many cases

IT ISN'T ROBBING THE KIDS

Another reason that people do less than they could is that they feel the charity they should support is their own family. They will give to their kids. In the next chapter, we'll take a look at how much is too much to leave to your children. Are they really your best "charity"?

For one thing, they will not be treated as a charity for tax purposes. And as I have already shown, you can do both: support a charity and your family too without anyone sacrificing. Also, you can involve charity in the manner in which you leave money for your children. The charity can get it for a while, and then your children can get it as part of a retirement plan when they are older.

Because many of us will live a lot longer than generations have in the past, people are concerned about running out of money. And there are, indeed, plenty of other concerns they could have: Are they going to get sick? Is anyone going to sue them? Are their heirs mature enough to handle an inheritance? What about the prospect of a divorce? What's going to happen to the tax system? All of those considerations can be analyzed and quantified, and we can determine whether some of these charitable techniques can help in increasing income for a longer period of time, not only for you but also for your children and grandchildren.

WHY PEOPLE PUT IT OFF

Even when people are convinced they could do more, they often procrastinate. It is not a lot of fun to think about numbers. There are plenty of other things to fill up your day. Nor is it pleasant to think of your mortality. To talk about who will get your estate means you have to confront the prospect of your passing. That's something people tend not to want to broach. I think we all know we cannot be here forever, but that doesn't mean we want to be reminded of the fact.

When you get older and you see friends and relatives taking ill or dying, you tend to think more about these issues. But people still put it off. It is human nature. Sometimes people are embarrassed about whether they have accomplished anything, and so they plan for nothing. As a result, widows and children are shocked to find out that what they thought had been arranged was not the case at all.

Also, it can be difficult to talk about estate matters because doing so can raise the heat on family issues that have long been simmering. It may be a matter of how to treat the children equitably, when it is apparent that some are more deserving than others. "As soon as I raise this issue," some think, "there's going to be a fight with my spouse, and I really do not want to go there." But if you're not going to resolve these things now, just when do you think you will? Is avoiding that fight really worth giving it to the IRS?

Just what is the cost of your procrastination? There is a cost to doing nothing, and many times it can be substantial.

You have to take a hard look at some things and make some decisions about matters that you would rather not think about.

Some people lack even a basic financial plan and have made no provisions for retirement. Perhaps they think they might have enough, but "might" is not good enough. You can't settle for guessing you will be all right. You have to know. And many people just do not know. They do not have a clear idea of how much they have and whether it will be enough, and that leads them to fear the worst. They have procrastinated on so many aspects of their financial life that charitable giving is just one more thing that they cannot see clearly. How are they going to look into that when they have yet to do the basics?

GETTING A CHECKUP

It is all curable to the extent that it can be defined. We can reduce it to numbers. It is like knowing your cholesterol count. You are either in fine shape or you are borderline or you are in horrible shape. Once you know the numbers, the next step is knowing what to do about it. What if you delayed retirement for a while? What if you saved more? What if you got a return on your investments that was more than you have been getting? All of that can factor into it, and charitable giving can help you as well with more income and less tax.

Again, you can project what your assets will do over time under a variety of scenarios. You can get a good grasp of what you need to do. To financial professionals, this is not voodoo. It is very basic, and they know the remedies, just like the doctor who knows what actions to take when your cholesterol numbers are over a certain range. We know what actions to take depending on the range of your cash-flow numbers.

A SAMPLING OF STRATEGIES

Let me offer you a sampling of strategies to think about so you can get a taste of the possibilities.

CHARITABLE GIFT ANNUITY

A charitable gift annuity is a simple way to supplement your retirement income and get a current tax deduction. It's very easy. This is not some complicated arrangement that requires a lawyer. Many charities make these available. Financial institutions make them available.

Basically, in its simplest form, you turn over cash. It can be other property, but in its simplest form, let's say you have money in a certificate of deposit, and today you are earning less than 1 percent. If you are around age 65, you could take that out of the bank, buy a charitable gift annuity, and immediately increase that income more than fourfold.

The income immediately goes up substantially for the rest of your life and you get a current income-tax deduction based on your age. Know that, eventually, that money will go to charity, so you should make this decision in the context of other elements of your financial plan. But if you need income, that's a simple way to do things. It is going to pay income for as long as you and your spouse live. You will get a substantially better payment than you would with CDs, which, historically, have failed to keep up with inflation. And you also get a tax deduction. But when you and your spouse pass on, the money goes to charity. That's why you're getting the tax deduction.

A GIFT OF STOCK

Another strategy that people use is the gift of stock. Let's say you have a gain in a stock. You could sell it, pay the tax, and make your gift to charity with the cash. But instead, you could choose to make the stock itself your gift to charity. You get the full benefit of that gift as a tax deduction, but you do not pay the capital gains tax. You are getting tax leverage there.

In other words, you might have paid $500 for the stock, and it is now worth $1,000 and you give it to charity. That's a full $1,000 deduction. Let's say 20 or 30 percent of that will be coming back to you due to the smaller tax bill. You get that full deduction for your gift without having to pay the capital gains on a stock that doubled in value.

DONATING YOUR HOUSE

Many people tell me that their house is not something their children want to inherit. If you are in that situation, why not consider donating your house to charity? Live in it for the rest of your life and get a current tax deduction for it. What will a charity do with a house when it gets it? It will sell it and realize the value at that time.

You might say that your family could do the same thing. But remember you are getting a tax deduction now for donating to charity. What are you going to do with that money? Let's say you get a $300,000 tax deduction. That could mean $100,000 back in your pocket, depending on your individual tax situation. Over time, you could accumulate that money in a trust or some account that would go to your family. By contrast, if you left that property to your kids and they did not want it, they would sell it. No tax exemption there. And there might be estate taxes and costs associated with that transfer to them.

LEAVE YOUR RETIREMENT PLAN TO CHARITY

One of the worst assets to die with is a retirement plan. An IRA, for example, could be taxed in your estate and then be subject to income tax paid by the person who inherits it. If you leave it to your children, they have to start taking the income out of it within a year, regardless of their age, and that income is going to be taxed. It is a horrible asset to retain in your estate. If you are planning to leave money to charity, consider donating the remainder of your retirement plan as one of the first sources of that bequest, which could be the most tax-efficient strategy for that money.

DONOR ADVISED FUND

Your decision to support a charity doesn't have to be irrevocable. You can change the beneficiary, and that happens sometimes.

When you are alive to see the results of your giving, you can do something about it. That is the benefit of current giving. According to an old rhyme, do your giving while you're living so you're knowing where it's going. However, you can also make sure your family continues to weigh in on charitable decisions while you are alive and long after you are gone.

You can do something as simple as a donor-advised fund. The family members get together each year—I know some who do this at Thanksgiving—and talk about a certain amount of money that will be given away. The money is in a donor-advised fund or in a trust or in a foundation. Each of the children can be commissioned with suggesting each year what should be done and why.

It is a great way to train the next generation not only in philanthropy but in due diligence. The family examines questions such as what the charity is doing with the money, why the family should give the money to that particular charity, how this money has been invested, whether the charity or the financial institution that is handling the investment is doing a good job and how the family knows this, and what the metrics are.

This is a great way to get the whole family involved. Many times it is a reason to bring everybody together. Imagine your family sitting around the holiday table, and the conversation is about a whole lot more than "pass the potatoes and pass the turkey." You're saying, "So Fred, John, Mary, what do you think about what the Salvation Army has been doing lately?" Your family is discussing the betterment of our world.

Do you need to have millions in assets to have such a conversation? No. You can do it with $10,000, not necessarily $10 million. You can set up a donor-advised fund with a financial institution or a community foundation that will take guidance from the family.

Let's say that $10,000 earned $1,000 over the last year. The family, together, can designate where those earnings go. You notify the financial institution or the community foundation, which will distribute the money to the charity you choose, unless you are told the charity doesn't qualify. "We've done our due diligence," the financial institution might say, "and it is not a charity we're comfortable giving money to. We do not think it would be a good investment for these reasons." Particularly if you choose a different recipient each year, that due diligence provides valuable information.

DONATING A LIFE INSURANCE POLICY

A lot of people have outdated life insurance policies. They might have taken them out when they were 35 years old and had young children. They took them out because if anything happened, the insurance money would take care of the spouse and get the kids educated. The children are now earning their own keep. The policy has outlived its original purpose. Rather than cash it in or just drop it, why not donate it? Here's another opportunity to leverage something substantial that might be several hundreds of thousands, or perhaps millions, of dollars.

You may or may not continue paying the premium. That's always an option. If you do, you can write a check to the charity for the premium and get a tax deduction for that amount. Or it could be an old policy that is paid up. But in any case, old insurance policies that no longer serve their purpose are a good place to look for charitable gift opportunities.

HOW AND WHEN TO GET STARTED

How do you get started? If you have a relationship with a charity, you contact the planned giving or development director of the charity. If your advisor has expertise in this area, you sit down with that person and go through the steps.

If your advisor has not presented any of these ideas, that would be one indication that either your advisor is not conversant in this area or is uncomfortable talking about it. In that case, you need to find a specialist in charitable wealth management. You want someone who knows his or her way around this area and who is known to the charities. The development folks at the charities probably know advisors. I would get input from more than one source. If you're talking to the charity, get your advisor involved. If you're talking to your advisor, get the charity involved.

You can learn some basic definitions online or from some of the financial institutions, but you need more than that. You could also get basic medical information online, but I would not want just anybody treating me. What you need is sound advice that is tailored to your situation. You need someone to take a close look to see whether what you have in mind for charitable giving makes sense for you.

Someone needs to run your numbers. We're very analytical here. The numbers will tell us whether a certain strategy makes sense. The numbers rule. After that, it is the client's decision on whether or not to take action, how to do it, how much to contribute, and where the money will go. You cannot make an informed decision, however, unless you have the "before" and the "after" written down in front of you. You need to clearly see the tax and financial impact of what you are contemplating.

When is the best time to leave assets to charity? I am a big believer in doing that while you are alive. Look at Joe. He got that increase in income right away, and he started increasing his giving as a result. It is much more satisfying to see the results of your giving while you are still around. And society most certainly benefits from the generosity of people in all walks of life. Those tax breaks for charitable contributions are in the IRS code for a reason. The government has an interest in encouraging such donations because of the redeeming benefits to society. Incentives for certain behavior are built into the code. For example, the mortgage interest deduction is there because we believe it is a great idea that people own their own home.

Likewise, you get a break for charitable giving because, as a people, we collectively believe it is a good idea to support those causes and institutions that do so much for all of us. Our society has a deep and abiding interest in making sure they flourish. That's why it is altogether possible within our system to reach out a helping hand to others while knowing we will have enough for ourselves.

CHAPTER 6

WHO MERITS YOUR MONEY?

M y friend Scott Keffer[2] tells the story of Oseola McCarty who had to quit school in the sixth grade to take care of an aunt in Hattiesburg, Mississippi. For decades she eked out a living washing clothes, and she often would walk a mile for groceries.

She died at age 91, in 1999, but not before leaving $150,000 to the University of Southern Mississippi to set up a scholarship fund

---

2 Scott Keffer is the founder of the Donor Motivation Program, in use by charities throughout the US and Canada to increase their planned giving results.

for students who otherwise, like her, would not have been able to go to college. The university awarded her an honorary degree for her philanthropy. The humble washerwoman was now Dr. Oseola McCarty.

She also bequeathed money to her church, and she left money to her niece and nephew. She saved it all, dollar after dollar, through years of toil. She washed clothes until she was nearly 90, when arthritis slowed her down.

To be proud of ourselves, she said, we must do things to be proud of. And despite her limited resources, she certainly did manage to do those things. Her gift might seem small compared to some endowments, but no one can deny it was a huge percentage of her heart. Each of us can strive to make a difference, even if we think we have little by comparison. It is the spirit that defines our humanity. We can leave a mark that lasts for generations.

When it came time for Oseola McCarty to seek financial counsel, an advisor spread ten dimes out in front of her. "If this represented all your money, where would you like each dime to go?" he asked her. And that's how she made her desires known. She slid one "dime" aside for her church and a dime each for her nephew and niece. And as for the rest? "I always wanted to teach but never could. I'd like all the rest to go to help kids go to college who wouldn't have a chance otherwise."

That's how a wise advisor can tap into a compassionate heart. Not only did he figure out how to communicate effectively, but he also got to the core of what she cared about. She cared about her church. She cared about her relatives. And that advisor gave her a clear way to express how much she cared about a cause.

Her story illustrates the essence of what this book has been about. She had the resources to make a difference. It certainly was not all the money in the world, but she was able to use it effectively. She left a great legacy. She left behind her life prints. She was a person of meager means and meager education who had a big heart and knew what she wanted to do.

GETTING READY FOR LIFE'S FINALS

When I talk to people and hear their stories, I learn a lot about what they truly care about. Those sentiments come naturally when people are getting older. You don't think about these things when you're 20, necessarily, when you are busy falling in love and raising a family and building a household.

There comes a time when you want to do more than accumulate. You want to distribute the bounty. You want to enjoy what you worked to acquire, of course, but part of the change in attitude is looking to see how you can do more than just take care of yourself.

That's a very natural part of life. It's as if you are studying for your finals in life. You are getting to the point of wondering why in the world you are here and what your life was all about. Was it gain for gain's sake? Was it for your family or for the family of man?

Some financial planners simply ask their clients, as if picking a question off a list, "So what about charity?" They check the "no" answer, and the matter is never addressed again. But we need to dig deeper. A lot of advisors are just plain uncomfortable discussing this area. When I talk to development people at charities, they explain that the uncomfortable advisors are the ones who lack a heart for charitable giving and lack experience. They have no history of involvement.

To me, it is very natural. I'm sure some advisors consider charity to be just something on a checklist, but that's not how the advisors I know think about it. You can always find out more about people by taking the time to ask them a few questions. You can address those same old fears that might result in their doing nothing.

I draw three interlocking circles on a napkin. The circles represent everything you own, and there are only three places where it can go someday. It can go to your family or other beneficiaries. It can go to the IRS, or it can go to charity. You get to choose. Unfortunately, when I ask the question, "What does this look like, currently, for you?" the most common response is "I don't know." And that, then, is where we start.

KEEPING UP WITH LIFE'S CHANGES

Sometimes people who think they're sophisticated will assure me that "it's all taken care of" and "I've got it all figured out." They feel certain about how much their family will get, how much charity will get, and how much the IRS will get, which they assert will be nothing.

Many times, when I examine the documents and analyze the numbers, all is not what they think.

That's not to say they did a poor job or failed to think things through. There are a lot of reasons for their misunderstanding. Their situation has changed, and so have the numbers. The family dynamic has changed. The tax law has changed. There can be a variety of reasons why the scenario differs from how it was a decade earlier or just a few years earlier.

Things may not be as they seem, so it always helps to have an updated view. We routinely do this for clients every six months, far more often than most people review their own documents. Regular reviews are crucial. Beneficiaries may need to change, for example, or the title to a property may be outdated. Perhaps making such changes was on a checklist at one point, but for whatever reason, they were not attended to. I can help make a difference. I can make sure that things get done.

WHEN FAIR DOESN'T MEAN EQUAL

Most people would, of course, want to leave money to their family rather than the government.

But do not presume that leaving a big pile of money to somebody is necessarily a loving thing to do.

Fair does not necessarily mean equal when it comes to children or grandchildren. That might be obvious, but many people divide an inheritance into equal shares. For example, three children will each get a third of the legacy.

However, one child might be a professional, a brain surgeon, perhaps. Another one might be a missionary in a third-world country. Should they be treated equally? Most people would say their shares should not be equal. Frankly, I find, in counseling families, that the siblings are fine with that. They understand.

The brain surgeon, for example, might say, "I'm fine financially, but my brother works like a dog and makes no money. I am going to have a retirement plan. I am going to be fine. But let's make sure he's okay." In the vast majority of cases in which I have been involved, the siblings don't expect an equal cut.

One of the siblings might clearly be far more adept at handling and preserving money, with a proven track record. Others might be spendthrifts. Most advisors know of people who are constantly asking for more money from their trust or parents and grandparents.

They just do not have a good grasp of budgeting and how long the money is going to last. It can be the best thing that ever happens to them when the terms of the trust dictate how the money can be spent. If they had free rein over it, other people easily could take advantage of them.

One child or grandchild could inherit a pile of money and be just fine with it. For another, it could be the worst thing that could happen. You need to carefully consider how such a distribution will be handled. It could be set up so that it is flexible. You do not have to completely tie it up, but over time, it will become obvious who can handle money and who cannot.

Maybe you have the next Bill Gates in your lineage, and that person needs to be encouraged. You can reward behavior. You can motivate behavior through bequests and legacy and testamentary arrangements, and you can withdraw money because of detrimental behavior.

You can be an encourager. You can use the money to advance people's lives. You can find a way to be fair even when you are dealing with differing levels of maturity and financial savvy. Certainly, if one of your children were mentally challenged, you would want to provide for that child in a fair way while still limiting control of assets to what is appropriate.

Or suppose it were obvious that one of your children or grandchildren was in a troubled marriage, perhaps on the verge of divorce. There are ways to protect that child and to keep the money away from a divorce claim.

Finally, you may have a child or other family member who has special needs because of a developmental disability. In such cases, you may want to assure that enough money is made available for them. This needs to be done so that any government benefits they are entitled to are not jeopardized by such inheritance. This is where a Special Needs Trust might be a suitable solution.

DIVVYING UP YOUR DIMES

Most people have some degree of charitable instinct. I mentioned earlier that you can get a glimpse of that just by looking at someone's checkbook and calendar. It is unusual to find somebody who has no desire to contribute.

When you start talking to people, you begin to understand what they care about. As you develop the relationship, you can sense whether they would be open to doing more. Many people do not get the opportunity to have someone show them how to leverage their resources to accomplish more. Feeling humble, they act humble. "It is just little old me," they say, but then, look at Oseola McCarty. Anyone who entertains the notion that charitable giving is just for millionaires and billionaires would do well to read again her story and look at her life as an example of the power of slow and steady work in pursuit of a dream.

I also point to the story of Oseola McCarty to show that there are ways to make more dimes from what you have. Make those dimes go further. Turn those dimes into quarters, perhaps, and dollars and more.

GIVING BACK

The neighborhood in Atlanta was so desolate that people referred to it as Little Vietnam. It had become a war zone. If a patrol car had occasion to enter, the officer would call for backup. The police would go in two-by-two because it was so dangerous.

One Sunday, local real estate developer Tom Cousins was reading an article about prisons in the *New York Times*. It reported that in the state of New York, the majority of inmates tended to come from a small number of zip code areas.

Cousins reached for the telephone, called the Atlanta Police Department, and posed the question, "Do we have this same situation here?"

"We do," the office told him. "And we can tell you it basically comes from one section of town."

"And where is that?"

"Little Vietnam."

He asked if an officer could take him down there for a look, and as they rode through the rough streets, he noticed a derelict golf course. It was a historically significant one, where Bobby Jones learned to play. Cousins is a golfer. He is currently a member of Augusta National, and he could see the potential there. The golf course could be the crown jewel around which he could rehabilitate the neighborhood and attract people back.

Cousins bought the course and set about working to bring new life to the area. He attracted investors and corporate sponsors and redid the club so that it was a nationally recognized place to play. The PGA Tour recently finished its tournament season with a prestigious golf tournament at the club.

And Cousins set up a K-12 school that emphasized good habits and manners. The kids who had been hanging out on the corners went to class in uniform and eventually headed out to find jobs. He gave them an entirely different model to which they could aspire.

The neighborhood is now a stylish place to be. Some young professionals live there as well as some people in government housing. The whole socioeconomic spectrum is represented there. It is south of the center of Atlanta.

Cousins' dream is to replicate this in despairing communities across the country. He wants to spread the word and advance a dream. He wants to give back in a grander way.

Businesspeople are problem solvers. I have found that some people are attracted to doing philanthropic work primarily because they've had a business career in which they were very accustomed to problem solving. They see societal issues that need to be addressed. It is very natural for them to make use of their experience and vision. They want to see how they can succeed where government has failed, not because its intentions were not good but because bureaucracy can be cumbersome.

Philanthropy is for the giver and for the receiver. It helps families, and it helps society. It is in the best interest of all of our communities. Enlightened individuals, Plato said, will conduct their affairs in search of wisdom and virtue to serve the greater good. All that they do is aimed at increasing the quality of life and the standard of living of everyone. If every individual were to operate with that view, what a better place this world would be.

We can contribute to that greater good with our time, our efforts, and our money. In giving financially, we are, in effect, giving all three, since money represents the fruit of our time and effort. When we share our money, we share ourselves. People are fond of the expression "filthy lucre," but it is only filthy lucre if it is used in a filthy way.

It is not just about money. Your legacy means more. We should share our values, our stories, our rich family histories.

The personal stories that you pass down will be how people remember you, generations hence. In the end, we want to leave our mark on this world. We want to leave our story, our life prints. You can leave a spiritual will, as well as a financial one, with letters and videos for your family.

Money is just a tool to accomplish a better life. It represents the essence of what we can provide and the total of what we built to give to others and in service to others. Once, a dollar represented gold. Now, it represents goods and services, the very things that we can provide to help other people.

As we give, so do we receive. It is true in a spiritual sense, and it is true in philanthropic planning since, as we have seen, giving and receiving are far from mutually exclusive. You do not need to shortchange yourself or your family by providing for the greater good. In fact, you likely will find that even more resources will come to you.

I too am very solution oriented. I do not like finger pointing. "Well, what is your solution?" I tend to ask when others look for the scapegoat du jour. To me, the real solution is to give of oneself. It is in the best interest of all of us that our communities thrive and prosper. That's the point of charitable giving.

Are you being a good steward? Are you using the resources that have come your way and managing them effectively for the benefit of all? Are you serving your money, or is it serving you? Those can be daunting questions, but many people truly want to contribute in a greater way. That's where I can help. I can show you the possibilities. You can do it. And once you know you can, why wouldn't you?

TO CONTINUE

FINDING YOUR

MONEY'S

GREATER PURPOSE

JOIN OUR E-MAIL LIST AT

MONEYSGREATERPURPOSE.COM

FOR TAX UPDATES, LEGACY PLANNING IDEAS, AND TIMELY TIPS.

Printed in the USA
CPSIA information can be obtained
at www.ICGtesting.com
JSHW012041140824
68134JS00033B/3198

9 781599 325798